OPTIONS STRATEGIES
EVERY INVESTOR
SHOULD KNOW

THE FINANCIAL LEXICON

"Be concerned only with the pure truth in what you read and not with the greatness or lack of learning of the author. Think more of what is said than of the one who said it."

Thomas à Kempis

Table of Contents

Why Publish Under a Pseudonym?

There are a few reasons I write under a pseudonym. First, I am of the opinion that neither academic nor professional distinctions make an individual a successful investor. I believe the investing community as a whole would be better served by focusing more time on the merits of an idea or investment thesis rather than simply assigning merit to an idea or investment thesis because of who said it or wrote it. Publishing under a pseudonym is my way of reinforcing that belief, as it allows the reader to focus on the topics discussed in this book rather than on the author.

Second, I am not seeking fame from my writing. I am not trying to win anyone's business, and I am not trying to sell any financial products. Moreover, what I write is not intended to act as investment advice. I am currently not interested in acting as either a financial advisor or a portfolio manager. Instead, I am more interested in presenting ideas and new ways of thinking about investing-related issues in an attempt to help individuals become the best informed investors they can be. I hope this book does just that, providing readers with helpful and actionable ideas for improving portfolio returns using options.

A Note to Readers

Whether you are an everyday investor interested in options trading or an experienced financial professional looking for a few helpful ideas, I hope you find this book useful. If you are an investor with less experience in the financial markets, I suggest reading this book from start to finish in the order it was written. If you are a financial professional well-versed in options terminology, you may want to skip Chapters 1 and 2.

In addition to this book, all investors should read *Characteristics and Risks of Standardized Options* prior to trading options. The PDF version of the booklet can easily be found on the internet and downloaded free of charge. You can also obtain one, free of charge, when you are approved for options trading by your broker.

Introduction

Risky. Dangerous. Speculative. Complex. Gambling. These are words you may have heard used to describe options trading. But here are a few other words I can use to describe options trading: sensible, income-enhancing, protection, helpful, risk-reducing. How can it be that words such as "risky" and "risk-reducing" both describe options trading? How can "dangerous" and "helpful" describe the same type of investing? What about "gambling" and "protection"? Those do not seem like two words that could represent the same type of investing. But they are.

If I were to tell you that investing in stocks is a dangerous, speculative, and gambling-like venture because some companies go bankrupt, sending their stocks to zero, you would probably tell me that I should not refrain from investing in stocks simply because some stocks go to zero. Investors who focus on large, well-established, multinational companies with strong brands and solid profits will likely experience portfolio returns that differ greatly from those who invest in small-cap companies that are losing money and burning through cash.

Similarly, if I were to tell you that when interest rates are near historic lows, investors should avoid fixed income securities due to the risk of price declines, those who own individual bonds could respond with a treatise about why that line of thinking need not apply to them. When the stock market has risen a lot and most stocks look expensive, there are often individual stocks that have bucked the trend, sold off, and are trading at enticing valuations. The same is true in the bond market. Even though interest rates may be near historic lows, investors can still find individual bonds with acceptable yields and acceptable credit risk. Furthermore, as long as an investor has the wherewithal to hold individual bonds to maturity, then daily changes in the prices of bonds become largely irrelevant.

Just as in the world of stocks and bonds, when it comes to options trading, there are different types of investors who use a variety of different strategies. Some people may execute those strategies that would be considered risky, dangerous, speculative, complex, or gambling-like. But those are not the only options strategies that exist. To disregard all options trading because there exist strategies that are not suitable for you would mean forgoing strategies that could help increase your income, get you out of a losing stock position, or allow you to purchase stocks at lower prices than the market is currently offering.

In this book, I present four options strategies that I think every investor should know. With an understanding of the strategies I describe, you will be better armed to protect and expand your wealth as you navigate the choppy investing waters of the world's financial markets. But before diving in and revealing the strategies, there are a few prerequisites we need to cover.

Let's get started!

CHAPTER 1

Prerequisites for Understanding The Four Options Strategies

Before describing the options strategies that are important for every investor to know, I want to make sure all readers of this book are on a level playing field in terms of basic knowledge about call and put options. I also think it is important that everyone reading this book has a basic understanding of a few concepts related to technical analysis. This will be helpful when executing the strategies outlined in this book.

What Are Options?

An option is a contract that, according to certain rules, allows for a specific financial instrument, called the "underlying," to be bought or sold at a specific price. For the purposes of this book, the underlying security will refer to a stock or an exchange-traded product (ETP).

There are two types of options with which you need to be familiar in order to eventually learn the soon-to-be-presented strategies: call options and put options.

Call Options

The owner of a call option has the right, but not the obligation, to purchase the underlying security at a particular strike price. Strike price refers to the price at which the option *owner* has the *right* to buy or sell a security. This is also the price at which the option *seller* (also known as the option "writer"), under certain conditions, has the *obligation* to buy or sell a security. As the seller of a call option, you might find yourself forced to sell shares of the underlying security.

An investor buying a call option would do so because of the expectation that the underlying security might head *higher* in price. But just because the underlying security heads higher does not necessarily mean the price of the call option will also head higher over time. A buyer of a call option is said to be "long" the call.

An investor selling a call option often does so because of the expectation that the underlying security will not close *above* the strike price that was sold. This is not always the case. But for the purposes of acquiring a basic understanding of options, remember that call sellers are, in a way, "short" the underlying security. Furthermore, a seller of a call option is said to be "short" the call.

Put Options

The owner of a put option has the right, but not the obligation, to sell the underlying security at a particular strike price. Again, strike price refers to the price at which the option *owner* has the *right* to buy or sell a security. This is also the price at which the option *seller* (also known as the option "writer"), under certain conditions, has the *obligation* to buy or sell a security. As the seller of a put option, you might find yourself forced to buy shares of the underlying security.

An investor buying a put option would do so because of the expectation that the underlying security might head *lower* in price. But just because the underlying security heads lower does not necessarily mean the price of the put option will head higher over time. A buyer of a put option is said to be "long" the put.

An investor selling a put option often does so because of the expectation that the underlying security will not close *below* the strike price that was sold. This is not always the case. But for the purposes of acquiring a basic understanding of options, remember that put sellers are, in a way, "long" the underlying security. Furthermore, a seller of a put option is said to be "short" the put.

Entering Options Orders for Execution

There are four types of transactions with which you should be familiar when entering an order to buy or sell an option:

1. When opening a new position (or adding to an existing position) by buying an option, enter a *"Buy-to-Open"* order.

2. When opening a new position (or adding to an existing position) by selling an option, enter a *"Sell-to-Open"* order.

3. When closing an existing position by buying an option, enter a *"Buy-to-Close"* order.

4. When closing an existing position by selling an option, enter a *"Sell-to-Close"* order.

Other Important Terms

In addition to understanding what call and put options are and what strike price and underlying security refer to, there are other important options terms that need to be discussed.

The *expiration date* is the date on which an options contract expires. Regarding monthly equity options, they expire on the Saturday immediately following the third Friday of the month. But you cannot trade on expiration day. Instead, the last opportunity to trade monthly options contracts is actually the day before, on the third Friday of the month. If the third Friday of the month happens to be a day the markets are closed, then the third Thursday of the month is the last opportunity to trade before expiration.

An *option chain* is a list of all available call and put options. The list includes all strike prices and expiration dates as well as the prices (premiums) at which the options are trading. Depending on the options platform you are using, it may also contain additional information that more advanced options traders will be interested in. An option chain could include weekly expiring, monthly expiring, and quarterly expiring options. Not every stock and exchange-traded product has an option chain. Stocks and exchange-traded products that do not have option chains do not have options available for trading. Moreover, just because a security has an option chain does not mean it will include weekly, monthly, and quarterly options. It could, for example, only have monthly expiring options, and those expiration dates might not be for consecutive months.

If you own a call or put option, you have the right to *exercise* the option. By exercising your right on a call option, you would purchase shares of the underlying security at the option's strike price. By exercising your right on a put option, you would sell shares of the underlying security at the option's strike price.

As a seller of an option (also known as an option "writer"), you open yourself up to an option *assignment*. In the case of a call option you are short, an assignment would result in your having to sell shares of the underlying security at the option's strike price. In the case of a put option you are short, an assignment would result in your having to purchase shares of the underlying security at the option's strike price.

The word *"premium"* is used to refer to the actual dollar amount (or other currency) paid or received for buying or selling an option. It can also refer to the price at which an option is trading.

An *in-the-money call option* refers to a call option strike price that is below the price of the underlying security. For example, if a stock is trading at $100 per share, the call option strike prices below $100 would be in-the-money.

An *in-the-money put option* refers to a put option strike price that is above the price of the underlying security. For example, if a stock is trading at $100 per share, the put option strike prices above $100 would be in-the-money.

An *out-of-the-money call option* refers to a call option strike price that is above the price of the underlying security. For example, if a stock is trading at $100 per share, the call option strike prices above $100 per share would be out-of-the-money.

An *out-of-the-money put option* refers to a put option strike price that is below the price of the underlying security. For example, if a stock is trading at $100 per share, the put option strike prices below $100 would be out-of-the-money.

In the example of a stock trading at $100 per share, the $100 call option and put option strike prices would be considered *at-the-money*.

Delta refers to the amount an option's price is expected to move for every $1 (or one point) change in the underlying security.

Theta refers to the rate of decline in an option's time value. This is also known as time decay.

Delta and theta are both members of what are known to options traders as the "Greeks." Other members of the Greeks, while important to advanced options traders, are beyond the scope of what I am hoping to convey in this book.

Three Additional Pieces of Information

First, it is important to remember that in most cases, options contracts represent 100 shares of the underlying security. On occasion, there are adjusted contracts that represent something other than 100 shares. An options trader should be able to tell that a contract is adjusted based on the symbol. A novice options trader who wants to be absolutely certain that an option represents 100 shares of the underlying security should call his or her broker.

Second, options have more complex looking symbols than investors may be used to. While stocks, exchange-traded products, and mutual funds have three to five letters in their symbols, options symbols are longer and include both letters and numbers. But even though an option's symbol is long and complex looking, its construction is relatively easy to understand. What follows is an example of an option's symbol and an explanation of its construction. Your broker may simplify it a bit by removing superfluous zeros.

XYZ151231C00100000

Perhaps you are thinking, "Okay, I've had enough of options now." I know the symbol looks like a jumbled mess. But it is really not as complex as it looks. Here is a breakdown of its construction:

XYZ151231C00100000 – XYZ represents the *ticker symbol* for the underlying security. The ticker symbol for the underlying will be at the beginning of an option's symbol.

XYZ**15**1231C00100000 – 15 represents the *year* of expiration. In this case, it is the year 2015. Only the last two digits of the year are used in an option's symbol.

XYZ15**12**31C00100000 – 12 represents the *month* of expiration. In this case, it is the month of December.

XYZ1512**31**C00100000 – 31 represents the *date* of expiration. In this case, it is the 31st day of the month.

XYZ151231**C**00100000 – "C" stands for call option. If this option were a put, a "P" would be used instead of a "C."

XYZ151231C**00100**000 – "00100" represents the strike price's dollar amount (no fractions of a dollar). In this case, it refers to the $100 strike price. The portion of an option's symbol that represents the strike price's dollar amount is officially five digits. But your broker may shorten it to remove zeros it deems superfluous.

XYZ151231C00100**000** – "000" represents the decimal portion of a strike price. In this case, there is no decimal attached to the $100 strike price. If we were discussing a $15.50 strike price, the three digits at the end of the symbol would be

"500." The portion of an option's symbol that represents the strike price's decimal amount is officially three digits. But your broker may shorten it to remove zeros it deems superfluous.

When you are trading options on your broker's platform, rather than seeing the long symbol XYZ151231C00100000, you might instead see something like this: XYZ151231C100. This is an example of the superfluous zeros being removed. If we were to change the strike price to $15.50 from the 100 used in the example, a shortened symbol might look like this: XYZ151231C15.5. Notice the decimal in the new example.

Finally, before moving on to an explanation of the four options strategies, it is important to have a basic understanding of an option's intrinsic value and its time value. In a nutshell, intrinsic value represents the actual value of an option. For call options, it is calculated by subtracting the strike price of an in-the-money call from the price of the underlying security. For example, if XYZ stock is trading at $100 per share, the intrinsic value of the $75 call option is $25 ($100 minus $75). For put options, intrinsic value is calculated by subtracting the price of the underlying security from the strike price of an in-the-money put. For example, if XYZ stock is trading at $100 per share, the intrinsic value of the $125 put option is $25. ($125 minus $100). At-the-money and out-of-the-money options have *no* intrinsic value.

Time value refers to the premium above the intrinsic value that is built into an option's price. At expiration, the time value of an option will be zero. If XYZ stock is trading at $110 per share, and the $100 *call option* is being offered for $15, the time value is $5. This is calculated in the following way:

$110 (underlying security price) - $100 (strike price) = $10 (intrinsic value)

$15 (offer price) - $10 (intrinsic value) = $5 (time value)

Additionally, if XYZ stock is trading at $110 per share, and the $120 *put option* is being offered for $20, the time value is $10. This is calculated in the following way:

$120 (strike price) - $110 (underlying security price) = $10 (intrinsic value)

$20 (offer price) - $10 (intrinsic value) = $10 (time value)

Technical Analysis

Technical analysis (TA) refers to the examination of price and volume data in order to try to predict future price movements. This book is not meant to provide a detailed examination of technical analysis. Instead, I merely want to provide a basic background of a few concepts, so that readers can utilize them when trading options in a real portfolio.

While I am not a believer that technical analysis can predict price movements many years into the future, I do think that certain concepts within technical analysis have credibility over shorter time periods. Three of my favorite pieces of technical analysis are moving averages, trend lines, and noteworthy highs and lows, all of which I use to determine support and resistance levels for a security. In my experience, using moving averages and support and resistance levels as supplements to your fundamental analysis of a security's worth can be very helpful in determining what your entry and exit points should be.

Moving averages are a representation of the average value of a security over a period of time. Popular moving averages include the 10-, 20-, 50-, 100-, and 200-day. I like to use them as trend-following indicators and as support and resistance indicators. Other types of support and resistance indicators I use include trend lines and noteworthy highs and lows. When drawing a trend line on a chart, investors typically connect the highs of an extended price move or the lows of an extended price move to form the line. Even though a stock's price does not always bounce perfectly off a trend line, it often comes close, providing opportunities for investors to buy or sell the stock with more confidence about the near-term price direction. Charting software provided by your broker or found on a variety of financial and investing websites make calculating moving averages and drawing trend lines a piece of cake. By noteworthy highs and lows, I am referring to prices at which a security topped out or stopped falling for an extended period of time. Often times, those prices will act as support (the lows) or resistance (the highs) levels on numerous occasions. When utilizing noteworthy highs and lows to determine resistance or support levels, it is important to keep in mind that the exact price you are watching should be monitored with some flexibility. Prices rarely bounce exactly off a support or resistance level. Once they get in the ballpark, you should be ready to act.

* * * * *

There is one more step to complete before describing the four options strategies that every investor should know. That step is to test your knowledge of the options-related material discussed in this chapter.

CHAPTER 2

Testing Your Options Knowledge

In order to more easily understand the options strategies I will soon present, you should have a decent grasp of the terms and concepts presented in Chapter 1. To help test your options knowledge, I have prepared the following questions—answer key follows.

1. XYZ stock is trading at $12 per share and has an option chain. In this case, the "underlying" refers to:

    a. XYZ
    b. $12 per share
    c. The owner of XYZ stock
    d. The option chain

2. The owner of a call option has:

    a. The obligation to purchase the underlying security
    b. The obligation to sell the underlying security
    c. The right, but not the obligation, to purchase the underlying security
    d. The right, but not the obligation, to sell the underlying security

3. Under certain conditions, the writer of a call option has:

    a. The obligation to purchase the underlying security
    b. The obligation to sell the underlying security
    c. The right, but not the obligation, to purchase the underlying security
    d. The right, but not the obligation, to sell the underlying security

4. The owner of a put option has:

   a. The obligation to purchase the underlying security
   b. The obligation to sell the underlying security
   c. The right, but not the obligation, to purchase the underlying security
   d. The right, but not the obligation, to sell the underlying security

5. Under certain conditions, the writer of a put option has:

   a. The obligation to purchase the underlying security
   b. The obligation to sell the underlying security
   c. The right, but not the obligation, to purchase the underlying security
   d. The right, but not the obligation, to sell the underlying security

6. If XYZ stock is trading at $50 per share, then:

   a. The $40 call option is in-the-money
   b. The $55 call option is in-the-money
   c. Both A and B
   d. Neither A nor B

7. If XYZ stock is trading at $75 per share, then:

   a. The $70 put option is out-of-the-money
   b. The $80 put option is in-the-money
   c. Both A and B
   d. Neither A nor B

8. The expiration date is the date . . .

    a. The underlying stock goes to zero
    b. Your broker closes your account
    c. On which the options contract expires
    d. None of the above

9. If you are the owner of an option, you:

    a. Have the right to exercise the option
    b. May be subject to an assignment
    c. Both A and B
    d. Neither A nor B

10. If you are the writer of an option, you:

    a. Have the right to exercise the option
    b. May be subject to an assignment
    c. Both A and B
    d. Neither A nor B

11. Typically, one options contract represents how many shares of the underlying security?

    a. 1
    b. 10
    c. 100
    d. 1000

12. Choose the answer that best describes the following option symbol: XYZ140307P00030500

   a. XYZ's July 3, 2014 expiring $30.50 put option
   b. XYZ's March 7, 2014 expiring $30.50 put option
   c. XYZ's July 3, 2014 expiring $305 put option
   d. XYZ's March 7, 2014 expiring $305 put option

13. Choose the answer that contains two option symbols referring to the same option contract:

   a. XYZ151231C00100000, XYZ151231P100
   b. XYZ151231C00100000, XYZ151231C100.5
   c. XYZ151231P00100000, XYZ151231P100.5
   d. XYZ151231P00100000, XYZ151231P100

14. In the world of options, delta refers to:

   a. Your favorite sorority
   b. The amount an option's price is expected to move for every $1 (or one point) change in the underlying security
   c. Time decay
   d. None of the above

15. XYZ stock is trading at $50 per share. The $40 call option is being offered for $12. What is the time value of the $40 call option?

   a. $40
   b. $12
   c. $10
   d. $2

16. XYZ stock is trading at $20 per share. The $15 put option is being offered for $0.25. What is the time value of the $15 put option?

   a. $15
   b. $5
   c. $0.25
   d. $0

17. XYZ stock is trading at $85 per share. The $90 call option is being offered for $1.50. What is the intrinsic value of the $90 call option?

   a. $85
   b. $5
   c. $1.50
   d. $0

18. XYZ stock is trading at $65 per share. The $75 put option is being offered for $13. What is the intrinsic value of the $75 put option?

   a. $75
   b. $13
   c. $10
   d. $3

19. In the world of options, strike price refers to:

   a. The price at which the option owner has the right to buy or sell the underlying
   b. The price at which the option seller, under certain conditions, has the obligation to buy or sell the underlying
   c. The price at which an option contract can be exercised
   d. All of the above

20. If you were short a put option and wanted to close the position, you would enter what type of order?

   a. Buy-to-open
   b. Buy-to-close
   c. Sell-to-open
   d. Sell-to-close

1. XYZ stock is trading at $12 per share and has an option chain. In this case, the "underlying" refers to:

   a. XYZ
   b. $12 per share
   c. The owner of XYZ stock
   d. The option chain

2. The owner of a call option has:

   a. The obligation to purchase the underlying security
   b. The obligation to sell the underlying security
   c. The right, but not the obligation, to purchase the underlying security
   d. The right, but not the obligation, to sell the underlying security

3. Under certain conditions, the writer of a call option has:

   a. The obligation to purchase the underlying security
   b. The obligation to sell the underlying security
   c. The right, but not the obligation, to purchase the underlying security
   d. The right, but not the obligation, to sell the underlying security

4. The owner of a put option has:

   a. The obligation to purchase the underlying security
   b. The obligation to sell the underlying security
   c. The right, but not the obligation, to purchase the underlying security
   d. The right, but not the obligation, to sell the underlying security

5. Under certain conditions, the writer of a put option has:

   a. The obligation to purchase the underlying security
   b. The obligation to sell the underlying security
   c. The right, but not the obligation, to purchase the underlying security
   d. The right, but not the obligation, to sell the underlying security

6. If XYZ stock is trading at $50 per share, then:

   a. The $40 call option is in-the-money
   b. The $55 call option is in-the-money
   c. Both A and B
   d. Neither A nor B

7. If XYZ stock is trading at $75 per share, then:

   a. The $70 put option is out-of-the-money
   b. The $80 put option is in-the-money
   c. Both A and B
   d. Neither A nor B

8. The expiration date is the date . . .

    a. The underlying stock goes to zero
    b. Your broker closes your account
    c. On which the options contract expires
    d. None of the above

9. If you are the owner of an option, you:

    a. Have the right to exercise the option
    b. May be subject to an assignment
    c. Both A and B
    d. Neither A nor B

10. If you are the writer of an option, you:

    a. Have the right to exercise the option
    b. May be subject to an assignment
    c. Both A and B
    d. Neither A nor B

11. Typically, one options contract represents how many shares of the underlying security?

    a. 1
    b. 10
    c. 100
    d. 1000

12. Choose the answer that best describes the following option symbol: XYZ140307P00030500

    a. XYZ's July 3, 2014 expiring $30.50 put option

    b. XYZ's March 7, 2014 expiring $30.50 put option

    c. XYZ's July 3, 2014 expiring $305 put option

    d. XYZ's March 7, 2014 expiring $305 put option

13. Choose the answer that contains two option symbols referring to the same option contract:

    a. XYZ151231C00100000, XYZ151231P100

    b. XYZ151231C00100000, XYZ151231C100.5

    c. XYZ151231P00100000, XYZ151231P100.5

    d. XYZ151231P00100000, XYZ151231P100

14. In the world of options, delta refers to:

    a. Your favorite sorority

    b. The amount an option's price is expected to move for every $1 (or one point) change in the underlying security

    c. Time decay

    d. None of the above

15. XYZ stock is trading at $50 per share. The $40 call option is being offered for $12. What is the time value of the $40 call option?

    a. $40

    b. $12

    c. $10

    d. $2

16. XYZ stock is trading at $20 per share. The $15 put option is being offered for $0.25. What is the time value of the $15 put option?

    a. $15
    b. $5
    c. $0.25
    d. $0

17. XYZ stock is trading at $85 per share. The $90 call option is being offered for $1.50. What is the intrinsic value of the $90 call option?

    a. $85
    b. $5
    c. $1.50
    d. $0

18. XYZ stock is trading at $65 per share. The $75 put option is being offered for $13. What is the intrinsic value of the $75 put option?

    a. $75
    b. $13
    c. $10
    d. $3

19. In the world of options, strike price refers to:

    a. The price at which the option owner has the right to buy or sell the underlying

    b. The price at which the option seller, under certain conditions, has the obligation to buy or sell the underlying

    c. The price at which an option contract can be exercised

    d. All of the above

20. If you were short a put option and wanted to close the position, you would enter what type of order?

    a. Buy-to-open

    b. Buy-to-close

    c. Sell-to-open

    d. Sell-to-close

Once you are comfortable enough with the material presented thus far in the book, please continue to Chapter 3 where you will learn the first of the four options strategies every investor should know.

CHAPTER 3

Covered Calls

The first strategy I would like to present is among the most basic of the bunch. But just because it is simple in its construction does not minimize its importance. Selling covered calls is an excellent way to bring in income for your portfolio. If you patiently and judiciously execute a strategy of continually selling covered calls over extended periods of time, you can absolutely enhance returns in your portfolio. With that said, I would like to remind readers of the often repeated saying among investors, "There is no such thing as a free lunch." There are risks involved with each of the options strategies I will present, including selling covered calls, just as there are risks in every other investment you make. One of the keys to investing successfully over a period of many years is to understand the risks involved in an investment you are considering and to judge whether, in your particular situation, the risks outweigh the benefits. In the pages that follow, I will do my best not only to explain each of the four options strategies but also to describe some of the risks involved with each.

There are two parts to creating a covered call position in your portfolio: First, you must own a security like a stock or exchange-traded product. Second, you must sell a call option for which the security you own is the underlying security. For example, if you own XYZ stock, to create a covered call position, you would sell a call option on XYZ's option chain.

Remember that as the seller of a call option, you have the obligation to sell shares of the underlying security if the call option you are short closes in-the-money on expiration day. You would also have to sell shares of the underlying if the owner of a call option exercises his or her right to purchase shares and your calls are chosen for assignment. An in-the-money close on expiration day would result in an auto-assignment, known as "exercise by exception." But as long as you own shares of the underlying security, then you are "covered" should the call option you wrote be assigned—hence the name "covered call."

Before continuing on, I would like to make sure you understand what a covered call option is by asking the following question:

Which of the following positions includes a covered call?

    a. XYZ stock purchased at $30
    b. XYZ stock purchased at $20 and an XYZ short put position at the $18 strike
    c. XYZ stock purchased at $50 and an XYZ long call position at the $55 strike
    d. XYZ stock purchased at $40 and an XYZ short call position at the $45 strike

The correct answer is "D." Answer "A" cannot be a covered call position because there is no option attached to the stock position. Answer "B" is not correct because the position involves a put option rather than a call option. Answer "C" is incorrect because the position pairs a stock position with a long call position. Answer "D" is correct because covered call positions involve owning a stock and selling a call option. When you sell a call option, you are "short" the call.

Why might you want to sell a covered call? You would want to sell a covered call because you are paid for taking on the risk of having to sell your shares at the strike price at which you sold the covered call. The amount you are paid depends on a variety of factors and, in some situations, can be quite an enticing amount. For illustrative purposes, let's look at a few real world examples.

Real World Examples

On May 22, 2013, the State Street Global Advisors SPDR S&P 500 ETF, ticker symbol SPY, closed at $165.93 per share. Let's pretend you own 500 shares of SPY that you purchased at $100 per share. If you were interested in creating a covered call position with SPY, you might consider selling five of the June 22, 2013 expiring $167 calls for $1.81 per share (each contract represents 100 shares of SPY).

Since this is the first time I am giving a real world example of a price at which you would buy or sell a security, I would like to briefly add the following important pieces of information: First, I am of the opinion that market orders should only be used in extremely rare circumstances and *never* when buying or selling options. Instead, I prefer to use limit orders, which allow investors to enter the worst price at which they are willing to buy or sell a security. Second, for a sell order, the price at which you can theoretically receive an immediate order execution will be displayed on the "Bid." For a buy order, the price at which you can theoretically receive an immediate order execution will be displayed on the "Ask." The ask price is also sometimes referred to as the offer price. If you would like to virtually guarantee yourself an immediate order execution on a sell order, place a sell limit order at the bid price. Conversely, if you would like to virtually guarantee yourself an immediate order execution on a buy order, place a buy limit order at the ask price.

I used the words "theoretically" and "virtually guarantee" for two reasons: First, your order size might be too big for the amount of shares available at the bid price or the ask price. In that case, you might only receive a partial execution on your order. Second, it is possible the bid and ask prices of the security you want to trade change before you have time to enter your limit order. In order to increase the odds of order execution using a limit order, you could enter a buy limit order at a price slightly higher than the most recent offer price or a sell limit order at a price slightly lower than the most recent bid price. This would help compensate for the time between when you are filling out your order and when the order is submitted to the market for execution. If you want to completely avoid the risk of not being filled on a limit order, you can always place a market order (but do so at your own peril in the options market). Market orders are supposed to be filled at the next best available price.

Turning back to the covered call example, by selling five June 22, 2013 expiring $167 SPY call options for $1.81, you would collect $1.81 per share (not per contract) for taking on the risk of possibly having to sell your shares at $167. This means you would collect $905 before commissions and would have to sell your shares should SPY close above $167 on expiration (one month later). If SPY does not close above $167 on expiration, you would keep the entire premium, and your obligation under the option contracts would expire. If SPY closes above $167 on expiration, you would still keep the entire premium, but you would also have to sell your shares at $167. Under that scenario, you would have effectively sold your shares for $167 per share plus the $1.81 per share you collected in option premiums less commissions.

The premium of $905 might not sound like a lot, but let me remind you that it represents 1.81% of your cost basis ($100 per share) and 1.09% of the then-current price of SPY ($165.93 per share). Furthermore, you would receive that premium for taking on just one month's worth of risk and would only have to sell your shares if SPY closed above $167 on expiration.

Should you be interested in higher premiums and think the S&P 500 (SPY) were heading lower over the near term, you might also consider selling five June 22, 2013 expiring $165 calls. On May 22, 2013, they were slightly in-the-money and garnered the bigger premium of $2.91 per share. Selling five contracts at $2.91 would result in a premium of $1,455 before commissions. Moreover, if you felt comfortable enough going out to the end of the year, you could sell five December 31, 2013 expiring $169 call options for $5.57. Selling five contracts at $5.57 would result in a premium of $2,785 before commissions.

The aforementioned SPDR S&P 500 ETF, SPY, is a fund representing a broad basket of stocks. If you want to narrow your focus to a particular industry or stock, it is possible to collect much larger premiums than those offered by SPY. After already having declined on a consistent basis for well over a year, gold mining stocks experienced a horrific selloff during the early part of April 2013. The Van Eck Global Market Vectors Gold Miners ETF, ticker symbol GDX, dropped 28% from its $37.88 April 1, 2013 high to its $27.27 April 17, 2013 low.

The day following that low, GDX was offering roughly 5% call option premiums for investors willing to buy shares and sell slightly out-of-the-money covered calls expiring just four weeks later. On the other hand, if you were willing to buy shares at the April 18, 2013 closing price of $28.22 and hold those shares until December's expiration date, you could sell $29 call options for $3.20. That is an 11.34% premium, relative to the April 18, 2013 $28.22 closing price, for those investors willing to hold the shares for eight months. For investors willing to sell even further out-of-the-money calls, on April 18, 2013, the $33 December expiring strike had a premium of $1.87 per share. In other words, investors were being offered the opportunity to buy shares at $28.22, allow themselves the possibility for 16.94% appreciation in the shares (up to $33), and collect a premium of 6.63% (based on the cost basis of $28.22).

I hope these examples serve as good illustrations of the variety of premiums investors can collect when selling covered calls. Before describing some of the risks involved with covered calls, I would like to first address two questions you may have:

First, perhaps you are wondering, "Who would pay some of those premiums?" Market makers and investors willing to speculate on a rise in the share prices of SPY and GDX are the ones offering those premiums to willing call sellers. The size of the premium will be determined by a number of factors.

Second, some of you may be wondering if there are any helpful hints I have for selecting strike prices. To answer that question, I would like to explain why it is I chose the SPY $167 strike price as an example.

In May 2013, the S&P 500 and its corresponding ETFs (such as SPY) had broken out above the previous all-time high established in October 2007, soaring to new highs time and time again. Then, on May 22, 2013, the S&P 500 finally showed its first serious sign of weakness. On that day, the index first soared to a new high of 1,687.18, up more than 1% from the previous day's close, before things suddenly changed. The selling that commenced not only took away the day's gains, but eventually sent the S&P 500 down more than 20 points on the day (more than 1%) before closing the day down 13.81 points. If you were looking for a signal from the market regarding when the right time might be to sell a covered call, May 22, 2013 was it.

The outside reversal on May 22, 2013 gave covered call

writers easily-identifiable resistance levels on a chart. Those resistance levels can help covered call writers determine which strike prices are the most appropriate to sell. Incidentally, an outside reversal is a technical term for when both the highs and lows of the day exceed both the highs and lows of the previous day. On May 22, 2013, the highs and lows for the S&P 500 actually exceeded the highs and lows of the previous three trading sessions. If, around that time, you were looking for a reasonable strike price at which to sell covered calls, choosing a price right around or just above SPY's May 21 closing price of $167.17 would make sense. That level represented the all-time closing high for SPY and was achieved after a breathtaking multi-month rally for the major market averages. Once the rather large outside reversal on SPY's highest volume day in nearly three months took place, it was as good a time as any to sell covered calls.

Using very basic technical analysis as a guide for choosing a strike price is not a foolproof strategy, but it can often be quite helpful. More advanced technical analysis could also be done to determine a strike price for selling a covered call. But I am hoping to show throughout this book that even investors with less experience can incorporate a few simple steps to put the odds of investing success more in their favor.

Risks

The discussion of covered calls would not be complete without addressing some of the risks investors should keep in mind. First, if you are attempting to use covered calls as a hedge against an underlying position, remember that you are only hedging yourself by the amount of the premium you collect. The underlying security could decline by much more than the premium you collect. Additionally, prior to expiration, the underlying security could go much higher than the strike price at which you sold a covered call. You should therefore be comfortable with the possibility of leaving profits on the table.

Furthermore, there are tax considerations investors must keep in mind when selling covered calls. When choosing a strike price at which to sell a covered call, it is important to be comfortable with the fact that you might have your shares called away from you. When this happens, you could always repurchase the underlying security with the proceeds from the sale, but you would have to first pay taxes on any gains from the sale of the underlying. This would leave you less money with which to repurchase the shares. As a result, if the stock continues higher, you could lose out on future gains you would have had with the original, larger position.

Another tax consideration to be aware of concerns loss deferral rules, "Qualified covered calls," and holding periods. The tax code is not known for being easy to understand. I will do my best to simplify the tax rules that follow. But please keep in mind that I am not a tax advisor, and that you should refer to the appropriate IRS documents (Publication 550, for example) and qualified tax experts if you have any questions.

When you sell a covered call, you have created an offsetting position that the IRS considers a straddle. Straddles have a specific year-end loss deferral rule you will want to be aware of. In general, the purpose of the loss deferral rule is to prevent you from using offsetting positions to reduce your tax bill in the current year or push forward gains to the following year. If you have sold a "Qualified covered call," however, you can avoid the loss deferral rules. In order for an option to be considered a "Qualified covered call," all the following must be true (directly quoted from "IRS Publication 550: Investment Income and Expenses"):

1. The option is traded on a national securities exchange or other market approved by the Secretary of the Treasury.

2. The option is granted more than 30 days before its expiration date. For covered call options entered into after July 28, 2002, the option is granted not more than 12 months before its expiration date or satisfies term limitation and qualified benchmark requirements published in the Internal Revenue Bulletin.

3. The option is not a deep-in-the-money option.

4. You are not an options dealer who granted the option in connection with your activity of dealing in options.

5. Gain or loss on the option is capital gain or loss.

While all five rules are important, there are two in particular most investors will need to pay extra attention to—rules two and three. Concerning rule number two, when choosing your expiration dates, be sure you adhere to the limitations set forth in that rule. Regarding rule number three, let's define "deep-in-the-money option" using the wording found in IRS Publication 550: "A deep-in-the-money option is an option with a strike price lower than the lowest qualified benchmark (LQB)."

What is the LQB? "The LQB is the highest available strike price that is less than the applicable stock price." Publication 550 continues, "However, the LQB for an option with a term of more than 90 days and a strike price of more than $50 is the second highest available strike price that is less than the applicable stock price."

Perhaps not surprisingly, the tax code makes things fairly complicated. IRS Publication 550 continues, "If the applicable stock price is $25 or less, the LQB will be treated as not less than 85% of the applicable stock price. If the applicable stock price is $150 or less, the LQB will be treated as not less than an amount that is $10 below the applicable stock price." What is the definition of "applicable stock price"?

It is defined as "(1) The closing price of the stock on the most recent day on which that stock was traded before the date on which the option was granted; or (2) The opening price of the stock on the day on which the option was granted, but only if that price is greater than 110% of the price determined in (1)."

If the language I quoted from IRS Publication 550 is enough to make your head spin and scare you from using covered calls, you can avoid having to worry about the rules by only selling covered calls that expire 30 days or more before the end of a calendar year. If you sell any covered calls that expire within 30 days of the end of a calendar year or that expire in the following calendar year, you will want to not only review the tax rules just mentioned, but you will also want to review other rules in IRS Publication 550. Furthermore, you can avoid having to worry about the rules by only selling covered calls in a tax-advantaged account, such as an IRA.

Next, you should be aware of the implications of selling covered calls as they relate to holding periods. Your holding period of a stock or exchange-traded product determines whether your dividends and capital gains qualify for special long-term tax rates or whether they are taxed as ordinary income. For example, in order for dividends to be considered "qualified," you must have held the security for more than 60 days during the 121-day period that begins 60 days before the ex-dividend date. In the case of preferred stock that has not paid dividends for more than 366 days, and those dividends are eligible for the favorable tax rates, you must have held the stock more than 90 days during the 181-day period that begins 90 days before the ex-dividend date. *But your holding period can be suspended or eliminated during times when your risk of loss is diminished.*

The information in the following paragraph regarding suspended and eliminated holding periods is based on information found in two articles by BBD, LLC, a firm of Certified Public Accountants located in Philadelphia, Pennsylvania. The articles are called, "Tax Consequences Associated With Option Strategies – Part III," and "Tax Consequences Associated With Option Strategies – Part IV."

If you sell an *unqualified covered call* (deep-in-the-money) or an *in-the-money qualified covered call*, your holding period is suspended for the purposes of determining whether a dividend is qualified. The suspended holding period ends when the call option position is closed. For qualified covered call options that are out-of-the-money, the holding period is *not* suspended. Regarding capital gains that qualify as long-term, the holding period is *eliminated* should you sell an unqualified covered call (deep-in-the-money). For in-the-money qualified covered calls, the holding period is suspended while the call position is open. Out-of-the-money qualified covered calls are not subject to the suspension or elimination of the holding period. Much of this information can also be found in section 1092 of the Internal Revenue Code. The Internal Revenue Code is found in Title 26 of the United States Code.

Earlier, I noted that you can simplify your life regarding covered calls and taxes by only selling covered calls that expire 30 days or more before the end of a calendar year or by selling covered calls in a tax-advantaged account. Additionally, for simplification purposes, you might also consider focusing your covered call writing on out-of-the-money qualified covered calls (which are not subject to the suspension or elimination of holding periods) and on stocks that either do not pay dividends or just pay semiannual or annual dividends.

I would like to end the discussion of tax risks associated with covered calls on a positive note. When you sell a covered call, you collect the premium immediately upon settlement of your trade. You do not, however, owe taxes on that income when you receive it. Instead, you only owe taxes on that income when the position is closed (buy-to-close order on the covered call), the option expires, or, if an assignment takes place, when you sell the underlying stock. If you close the option position before expiration, any gain or loss would be considered a short-term gain or loss regardless of how long you held the position. If the option expires worthless, the gain would be considered short-term regardless of how long you held the position. Should an assignment take place, you would increase your proceeds from the sale of the underlying security by the amount you received when you sold the call option.

* * * * *

I realize the tax discussion related to covered calls is a tiring one. But before dismissing covered call writing as a possible strategy for your portfolio, keep in mind what I noted about ways to simplify your covered call tax experience. If, however, the tax discussion put a sour taste in your mouth regarding covered calls, I have another idea for how to bring in extra income in your portfolio using options—and its tax situation is much simpler. With that in mind, let's move on to the second of the four options strategies every investor should know: cash-secured puts.

CHAPTER 4

Cash-Secured Puts

The second strategy I will present is also quite basic in its construction and is an excellent way to generate income for your portfolio (in the form of short-term capital gains). But unlike with covered calls, initiating a cash-secured put position does not require owning the underlying stock. I am convinced that investors who master the use of cash-secured puts can, over extended periods of time, keep up with, if not exceed, the returns of broad-market equity indices. As I mentioned in the introduction to Chapter 3, there are risks involved with each of the options strategies I will present. After presenting the construction of a cash-secured put position and providing a real world example, I will present two overarching risks investors should be aware of when trading cash-secured puts.

Construction of the Position

There are a couple of different ways investors might consider using a cash-secured put option position. One such way is to sell put options with the hope of getting assigned the underlying stock at a price that is lower than that at which the underlying was trading at the time the option was sold. For the purposes of this book, I will focus on cash-secured puts that are sold with the hope that they expire worthless, not resulting in an assignment of shares. When you sell an option that expires worthless, you keep the entire premium and have no further obligation.

There is only one piece to the puzzle when creating a cash-secured put position: Sell a put option at the strike price and expiration date of your choice. Upon selling put options in a cash account, your broker will set aside an amount of money equal to the strike price multiplied by the number of option contracts multiplied by 100 (or, in the case of an adjusted contract, the correct amount of shares per contract). The money will be held by your broker until your obligation under the contracts expires, is closed by you, or, if assigned shares of the underlying, until the assignment takes place. Additionally, once your "sell-to-open" trade settles, your broker will deposit the premium owed to you into your account, and you can do with it as you please.

Selling cash-secured put options is often referred to as a strategy to be implemented when you are bullish (think prices will go higher) on a stock or index. But that is not necessarily the case. Selling cash-secured puts is a strategy that can be implemented both during times when you are bullish and during times when you recognize the risk of a possible bearish (prices heading lower) outcome. For example, if XYZ stock is trading at $40 per share, and you sell the $35 put option with the hope of the put expiring worthless, you will keep the entire premium as long as XYZ closes above $35 on expiration. In other words, the stock could decline by nearly 12.50% from where it was trading when the put was sold (a bearish outcome), and you would still keep the entire premium.

Remember that as the seller of a put option, you have the obligation to purchase shares of the underlying security if the put option you are short closes in-the-money on expiration day. You would also have to sell shares of the underlying if the owner of a put option exercises his or her right to sell shares of the underlying and your puts are chosen for assignment. An in-the-money close on expiration day would result in an auto-assignment, and you would own shares of the underlying security. You would pay for the shares using the cash originally set aside by your broker. Cash is held by a broker in order to ensure you have enough funds available to pay for shares of the underlying should an assignment occur—hence the name "cash-secured put."

Before continuing on, I would like to make sure you understand what a cash-secured put option is by asking the following question (you may want to review Chapter 1's "Entering Options Orders for Execution"):

Which of the following orders would result in a cash-secured put option after execution?

   a.   You sold-to-close an XYZ put option
   b.   You bought-to-close an XYZ put option
   c.   You sold-to-open an XYZ put option
   d.   You bought-to-open an XYZ put option

The correct answer is "C." Answers "A" and "B" cannot result in cash-secured put positions because sell-to-close and buy-to-close orders result in positions being closed. Answer "D" is not correct because the position involves buying a put option rather than selling a put option. Answer "C" is correct because cash-secured put positions are initiated by selling-to-open a put option.

Why might you want to sell a cash-secured put? You would want to sell a cash-secured put because you are paid for taking on the risk of potentially having to buy shares of the underlying. In other words, without ever having to buy a stock or exchange-traded product, you can collect premiums from the options market. Just as with covered calls, the amount you are paid depends on a variety of factors and, in some situations, can be a very enticing amount. Again, for illustrative purposes, let's look at a real world example.

Real World Example

On April 23, 2013, Rio Tinto, ticker symbol RIO, closed at $44.26 per share. Since its mid-February 2013 high of $58.90, the stock had pulled back nearly 25% in a little more than two months and was getting very close to multi-year support levels in the $39 to $43 region. Beginning on October 2, 2009, Rio Tinto's stock had found support in the $39 to $43 region on six occasions. These occurred in October 2009, May 2010, October 2011, June 2012, July 2012, and August 2012. If you were looking to sell cash-secured puts on a stock, from a basic technical analysis perspective, Rio Tinto looked attractive. But before deciding to sell puts on that company's stock, you would also have to consider a few other things.

Beyond a well-defined support region that makes choosing applicable strike prices an easier task, an investor looking to sell puts on Rio Tinto's stock would also want to examine the put premiums being offered to see if any are worth considering. As a general rule, remember that the closer an out-of-the-money strike price is to the current price of the underlying, the higher the put premium will be. An investor would therefore want to target as high a strike price as possible on Rio Tinto while also taking on as little risk as possible. To accomplish this, I would look at the $37.50 and $40 strike prices across different expiration dates. The $37.50 strike prices would be just below the major support region, and the $40 strike price would be at the lower end of the support region.

At the close of trading on April 23, 2013, the May 18 expiring $40 put options were bidding $0.25, and the May 18 expiring $37.50 puts were bidding $0.05. I would immediately dismiss the $37.50 puts as a viable choice because of the ultra-low premium. I would not, however, immediately dismiss the

$40 May 18 puts. The opportunity to collect 0.625% (excluding commissions) in less than four weeks at a strike price that is 9.62% below the current price of the underlying is something I would find tempting.

Next, let's take a look at the June 22 expiring options. On April 23, 2013, the $40 put options were bidding $0.80, and the $37.50 put options were bidding $0.40. That is a 2% and 1.07% return, respectively, in a bit under nine weeks on the money a broker would hold aside when selling those puts in a cash account (premium divided by strike price, excluding commissions). As mentioned in the previous paragraph, the $40 strike price was 9.62% below the then-current price of Rio Tinto's stock. The $37.50 strike price, on the other hand, was 15.27% below the then-current price of the stock.

Finally, let's look further out in time at the July 20 expiring options. On April 23, 2013, the $40 put options were bidding $1.20, and the $37.50 put options were bidding $0.70. That is a 3% and 1.87% return, respectively, excluding commissions, in a bit under three months on the money a broker would hold aside when selling those puts in a cash account. Again, the $40 strike price was 9.62% below the then-current price of Rio Tinto's stock, and the $37.50 strike price was 15.27% below the then-current price of the stock.

Here is a summary of the five possibilities in table form:

Expiration Date	Strike Price	Premium	Return
5/18/2013	$40.00	$0.25	0.625%
6/22/2013	$37.50	$0.40	1.070%
6/22/2013	$40.00	$0.80	2.000%
7/20/2013	$37.50	$0.70	1.870%
7/20/2013	$40.00	$1.20	3.000%

So which of the five different put options should we choose? Before answering that question, there is a bit more work to do. Besides thinking through which strike prices to consider and examining the premiums available on those strike prices, it is also important to keep event risk in mind. Even though event risk is not one of the two overarching cash-secured put risks I plan to address later in this chapter, it is an important risk to consider when choosing the appropriate expiration date and strike price for your trade. Event risk refers to any events that might occur that can cause large movements in the price of a security. Of course, some events could be impossible to predict, such as unforeseen corporate announcements or events that cause a market-wide crash. But others are known to market participants. These include upcoming corporate presentations at conferences, annual shareholder meetings, expected product announcements, and perhaps most importantly, earnings announcements.

The risk of selling a put before a stock-price-moving event such as an earnings announcement should not be overlooked. While options premiums in the month immediately following an earnings announcement are likely to be elevated due to the market attempting to price in expected volatility after the earnings announcement, you will need to be cautious when selling those puts. If you want to take the risk of selling puts with an expiration date in the weeks immediately following an earnings report, be sure you have done your homework on the company's likelihood of at least meeting investors' expectations. Furthermore, be sure to research prior historical moves for that company's stock price after earnings reports. This can at least help you better choose an appropriate strike price.

Next, let's work through which of the five aforementioned put options might be a good candidate for a cash-secured put.

In the case of Rio Tinto, it is expected to report earnings in the days just prior to July's expiration date. Given that, I would not want to take the chance of selling the July 20 expiring $40 puts, despite those puts having the highest premium of the five possibilities. Instead, if I were to sell a July put option, I would target a strike price below the support levels identified earlier.

Regarding the May expiring $40 option, even though it will provide a decent annualized return in a short period of time, the premium, on an absolute level, is rather small. If $0.25 per contract were all I was trying to capture in put premium, I might consider selling the June $40 puts for $0.80 with the intention of buying them back at a price of $0.55 during the next rally in Rio Tinto's stock price.

Now we are down to three remaining put options: the June $37.50, the June $40, and the July $37.50. When thinking about the performance of Rio Tinto's stock from mid-February through late April 2013 and combining that with the soft global economic data at that time, I would err on the side of caution when choosing the strike price at which to sell puts. After all, the goal is to have the put options expire worthless, freeing up your capital so you can sell more put options after the original ones expire. With that in mind, I will eliminate the July $37.50 puts, thereby removing the event risk of Rio Tinto's July earnings report.

The two remaining strike prices pose a challenge. Given the downtrend in the stock and the weak global macro data, my inclination is to remain more conservative and choose the $37.50 strike price. At the same time, I would want to utilize the multi-year support levels to bring in a decent premium. In my mind, there is no clear favorite between the June $37.50 and June $40 strike prices. Therefore, I would choose to split the position between the two strike prices.

If you do not have the capital to sell enough puts to make it worth your while to split the position (because the commissions would eat up too much of your premium), then I would consider doing this instead: Sell the June $40 puts for $0.80 with the intention of closing them at $0.20. A $0.60 profit on the entire position using the $40 strike price would be similar to selling half the position at the $37.50 strike for $0.40 and selling the other half at the $40 strike for $0.80.

One advantage to taking this route, besides saving money on commissions, is that you have the opportunity to capture the $0.60 profit prior to expiration. If you were to split the position as previously described, in order to capture the equivalent premium, you would need to wait for expiration and hope that all the options expire worthless. A disadvantage, however, to not splitting the position is that should the stock plunge below the $37.50 strike price, resulting in an assignment of shares, your cost basis on the non-split position would be $39.20 (excluding commissions), whereas your cost basis on the split position would be $38.15 (excluding commissions). Here is how to calculate the cost bases:

For the position entirely in the $40 strike price with an $0.80 premium, you simply subtract $0.80 from the strike price to get the cost basis. The strike price is the price at which you would have to purchase shares should an assignment occur, and the $0.80 is the premium you collected. The premium, for reasons I will soon explain, must be subtracted from the purchase price (strike price) when determining cost basis on a cash-secured put that received an assignment.

In order to determine the split position's cost basis, first calculate the cost basis of each portion of the position separately, add the two together, and divide by two.

The cost basis for the $40 strike price is $39.20 ($40 - $0.80), and the cost basis for the $37.50 strike price is $37.10 ($37.50 - $0.40). $39.20 added to $37.10 is $76.30, and $76.30 dividend by two is $38.15.

Why is put premium built into the cost basis of assigned shares? Once again, enter the tax code. This time, however, I am not including the discussion of taxes as a risk because in this case, it is a benefit.

Taxes

It is time to return to IRS Publication 550. But this time, I promise the stay will be short. When selling cash-secured puts, you collect the premium immediately upon settlement of your trade. You do not, however, owe taxes on that income when you receive it. Instead, you only owe taxes on that income when the position is closed ("buy-to-close" order on a cash-secured put), the option expires, or, if an assignment takes place, when you eventually sell the underlying stock. If you close the option position before expiration, any gain or loss would be considered a short-term gain or loss regardless of how long you held the position. If the option expires worthless, the gain would be considered short-term regardless of how long you held the position. Should an assignment take place on a short put position, Publication 550 has this to say:

"If a put you write is exercised and you buy the underlying stock, decrease your basis in the stock by the amount you received for the put. Your holding period for the stock begins on the date you buy it, not on the date you wrote the put."

As was previously illustrated in the Rio Tinto example, the option premium collected from selling the cash-secured put is therefore incorporated into the cost basis for tax purposes. If a cash-secured put you wrote eventually results in an assignment of shares of the underlying security, you would not owe taxes on the option premium collected from the put until the assigned shares are eventually sold.

Risks

In the opening paragraph of this chapter, I mentioned that there are two overarching risks to keep in mind when trading cash-secured puts. Before I discuss those two risks, I will mention a less significant risk, which should nevertheless be acknowledged.

When you are short a put option (or a call option for that matter), it is possible to be assigned even if the option is not in-the-money. It is a pretty rare event since a put owner does not have an incentive to exercise the puts on out-of-the-money options when he or she could simply sell the underlying security at a higher price in the open market. But technically you could be assigned on a put option you sold that is out-of-the-money.

Perhaps the biggest risk of this occurring is on expiration. If a put option closed just a fraction of a percent out-of-the-money on the last trading day prior to expiration, and a put holder believed the underlying security would drop below the strike price the following trading day, it is possible that the put holder would decide to exercise the option. Depending on the brokerage firm, there may be time for a put holder to exercise the option after trading closes on the last trading day before expiration but before the broker stops taking exercise instructions. Again, it would be a rare event for you to get assigned on an out-of-the-money option. Not only would someone have to first exercise a long put position, but your specific puts would have to be chosen for assignment from all the open short put positions at that strike price. If this were to happen to you, remember that getting assigned on an out-of-the-money put can end up being a positive thing for your portfolio. After all, you would get to purchase the underlying stock at a price lower than it would be trading at the time.

Now it is time to move on to the first of the two overarching risks of cash-secured put selling. First, the price of the underlying security might plunge to well below the strike price at which you sold puts. If this happens, you will still end up having to purchase shares of the underlying at the strike price you chose, which would be well above the price at which the underlying is trading on expiration. Beyond using basic technical analysis to choose your strike price, it is imperative that you spend time researching the financial stability of the underlying company (in the case of a stock). If you have done your homework on the fundamentals associated with the company and determined the company is sound, and you have chosen a strike price at which you are comfortable purchasing the stock, you should be able to survive the emotional aspects of having to purchase a stock at a higher price than it is trading when you make the purchase.

But even after surviving the emotional aspects of such a scenario, there is still the damage to the portfolio with which you will need to contend. Buy-and-hold type investors might decide to simply wait, giving the position time to recover. For those investors that prefer to take action, I will present a strategy in Chapter 6 to help you get out of this type of situation.

The second overarching risk to selling cash-secured puts is that the prices of the underlying security and broader-market indices could rocket higher. While this would cause your puts to expire worthless (exactly what you want to happen), as a put seller, your gains are limited to the premium you collected. Not only can it be frustrating to watch a security against which you hoped to sell puts for many months to come rocket higher in price, but if the broader market does so as well, it may be difficult to find other attractive put options to sell in the months that follow.

If selling cash-secured puts is a strategy that will take up a large percentage of your investable assets, you should make sure that identifying when to sell higher premium puts instead of lower premium puts becomes a strong skillset of yours. It would likely not feel very good to get left in the dust by the returns of the broader market because you were collecting 0.50% premiums instead of 2.00% premiums every few weeks while the major indices were in strong uptrends.

Should underperforming the major indices be a concern, you could also consider not holding short put positions to expiration. Instead, an alternative is to continually roll out of one put option into a higher strike as the price of the underlying moves higher. For example, if you sold puts at the $20 strike price when the stock was trading at $22.50, you could consider rolling into the $22.50 puts when the stock is around $25.30. This would maintain your buffer of slightly more than 11% between the price of the underlying security and your strike price while also ensuring you collect more in premiums during the stock's rise.

Another alternative, for those who are nervous about underperforming the broader indices with cash-secured puts, is to sell longer-dated put options that have higher premiums. This might include put options that expire more than a year in the future. Yet another way of addressing concerns about potential underperformance is to consider splitting a position between shares of the underlying stock and a short put position. You might even consider selling moderately out-of-the money covered calls against the shares you would own in a split position.

* * * * *

What would you say if I told you there was a strategy that allows you to collect immediate income without immediately owing taxes on that income, and, in a worst case scenario, have to purchase a security you would like to own at a lower price *at that lower price*? If that sounds like a strategy you would like to explore, then I have good news—you just did! Despite the risks associated with selling cash-secured puts, the ability to make money based on the performance of a stock or exchange-traded product without ever needing to own or short sell that security is something every investor should be aware of.

CHAPTER 5

Leverage Without Leverage

Among the four options strategies presented in this book, there is one that focuses on generating capital appreciation. Buying deep-in-the-money call options, a type of stock replacement strategy, allows investors to have high delta exposure to the price of the underlying security without having to own the underlying security. What do I mean by "high delta exposure"? Recall from Chapter 1 that delta refers to the amount an option's price is expected to move for every $1 (or one point) change in the underlying security. The deeper in-the-money you go on a call option, the closer the delta will be to one. And the closer the delta is to one, the more closely an option will track the price movements of the underlying security.

In addition, buying deep-in-the-money calls provides investors the opportunity to leverage a position without using leverage. What does "leverage without leverage" mean? The first "leverage" refers to increasing your exposure to the underlying security, while "without leverage" refers to doing so without using borrowed money. How is this possible? To answer this question, let's take a look at how a deep-in-the-money call option is constructed.

Construction of the Position

Investors hoping to closely track the price movements of an underlying security without having to invest the same amount of money as those who outright buy shares of the underlying should consider deep-in-the-money call options. As with cash-secured puts, there is only one piece to the puzzle of constructing a deep-in-the-money call option position: Buy a deep-in-the-money call option at the strike price and expiration date of your choice. After purchasing a call option, your broker will pull funds from your account to pay for the purchase. The amount withdrawn from your account will be equal to the price paid per contract multiplied by the number of contracts multiplied by 100 (or, in the case of an adjusted contract, the correct amount of shares per contract), plus commissions. For example, if you purchased three deep-in-the-money call options at the offer price of $30, it would cost $9,000 plus commissions ($30 offer price × 3 contracts × 100 = $9,000).

As the owner of call options, you have the right, but *not* the obligation to exercise the options and purchase shares of the underlying security. If you decided to exercise that right, you would have to pay an additional amount of money equal to the strike price multiplied by the number of contracts multiplied by 100 (or, in the case of an adjusted contract, the correct amount of shares per contract), plus commissions. In the example from the previous paragraph, if the call options purchased for $30 were the $50 calls, it would cost an investor an additional $15,000, plus commissions, to exercise the calls and purchase shares of the underlying security ($50 strike price × 3 contracts × 100 = $15,000). The cost basis in the shares purchased would be $24,000 before commissions ($15,000 from exercising the calls + $9,000 from purchasing the call options).

This is a good place to pause and ask a question that will test your understanding of concepts learned thus far in the book:

If you purchased the $50 strike price deep-in-the-money calls for a price of $30, and the time value in the options is $5, what is the current price of the underlying security, and what is the intrinsic value of the call options purchased?

    a.   Underlying security is $85; Intrinsic value is $30
    b.   Underlying security is $80; Intrinsic value is $25
    c.   Underlying security is $75; Intrinsic value is $30
    d.   Underlying security is $75; Intrinsic value is $25

The correct answer is "D." The price of the underlying security is calculated by adding the price of the call option to the strike price ($30 + $50 = $80) and then subtracting the time value ($80 - $5 = $75). The intrinsic value is calculated by subtracting the strike price from the price of the underlying security ($75 - $50 = $25).

Now let me answer the last question posed in the introduction to this chapter. How is it possible to "leverage without leverage"? If you purchase deep-in-the-money call options and use the funds that you saved from not purchasing the stock outright to purchase even more call options, you will have leveraged your position without using borrowed money. Here is an example:

You have the choice of buying 500 shares of XYZ at $75 per share or purchasing five $40 call options for $36. The $40 call options have a delta of 0.99. If you choose to purchase the shares, you will spend $37,500 before commissions. If you purchase five call options for $36, you will spend $18,000 before commissions, have unlimited upside to the position (just as the stock does), and track the price movements of XYZ almost to the penny. The delta of 0.99 means your options position should increase $0.99 for every $1 increase in the stock. This is where the leverage piece of the puzzle comes in. The difference between the $37,500 you were considering spending on shares of XYZ and the $18,000 it costs to purchase the deep-in-the-money call options is $19,500. You can take that money and purchase even more $40 call options, leaving you with far more exposure to XYZ stock than you would have had using the $37,500 to purchase shares.

In fact, with the additional $19,500, you could double your exposure to XYZ stock and still have $1,500 left over. This means you could have 1,000 shares of exposure through deep-in-the-money call options with a delta of 0.99 for less money than it would cost to purchase 500 shares of XYZ stock. It is in this way that you are able to leverage your position (additional exposure) without using leverage (borrowed money). There are certainly risks to doing this, and they will be addressed later in this chapter. But at this time, there is other business to attend to. Let's start by testing your knowledge of what a deep-in-the-money call option is.

Identify the deep-in-the-money call option(s) among the following positions:

a. XYZ's $50 call option when XYZ is trading at $90

b. XYZ's $50 call option when XYZ is trading at $45

c. XYZ's $40 call option when XYZ is trading at $40

d. XYZ's $40 call option when XYZ is trading at $70

e. None of the above

f. (A) and (B)

g. (B) and (D)

h. (A) and (D)

The correct answer is "H." Answer "B" is incorrect because the call option is out-of-the-money, and answer "C" is incorrect because the call option is at-the-money. Both answers "A" and "D" involve in-the-money call options that are certainly far enough in-the-money to be considered deep-in-the-money. Therefore, both "A" and "D" are deep-in-the-money call options, thus making "H" the correct answer.

You might be wondering how exactly to determine whether an option is "deep-in-the-money." If you remember from Chapter 3's tax discussion, IRS Publication 550 defines a deep-in-the-money option in this way: "A deep-in-the-money option is an option with a strike price lower than the lowest qualified benchmark (LQB)." Publication 550 then continues into far more specifics than are necessary for the purposes of this chapter. Instead, I would like readers to focus on the following four criteria for identifying a deep-in-the-money call option to serve as a stock replacement: (1) A strike price that is significantly in-the-money, (2) A call option with a delta of at least 0.90, (3) A call option with very little time value, and, (4) If you are interested in leveraging in the manner previously discussed, the strike price of the call option should be so far in-the-money that the odds of the price of the underlying security falling below it are very small.

As an options trader, for tax purposes, you still have to be aware of Publication 550's definition of deep-in-the-money. But that definition will not help you figure out how to properly construct this type of position in your portfolio. Therefore, for the purposes of executing this stock replacement strategy using deep-in-the-money call options, I will temporarily push the IRS definition aside.

Bank of America's stock, ticker symbol BAC, will serve as a good example for this stock replacement strategy. I would like to start by examining the November 16, 2013 expiring options. On April 24, 2013, with Bank of America's stock at $12.31, the offer prices on the in-the-money call options were as follows:

Expiration Date	Strike Price	Ask (Offer)
11/16/2013	$3.00	$9.35
11/16/2013	$4.00	$8.35
11/16/2013	$5.00	$7.35
11/16/2013	$6.00	$6.35
11/16/2013	$7.00	$5.40
11/16/2013	$8.00	$4.40
11/16/2013	$9.00	$3.50
11/16/2013	$10.00	$2.59
11/16/2013	$11.00	$1.82
11/16/2013	$12.00	$1.18

A basic overview of the call options shows there is a sufficient number of strike prices to choose from. It also shows offer prices that do not seem unreasonable given the stock's price of $12.31. But in order to go through the previously mentioned four criteria for selecting a deep-in-the-money call option to purchase, we will need additional information. Let's take a look at the same table with a few added pieces of critical information:

Expiration Date	Strike Price	Ask (Offer)	Time Value	Dividends Missed	Delta
11/16/2013	$3.00	$9.35	$0.04	$0.02	0.9916
11/16/2013	$4.00	$8.35	$0.04	$0.02	0.9895
11/16/2013	$5.00	$7.35	$0.04	$0.02	0.9871
11/16/2013	$6.00	$6.35	$0.04	$0.02	0.9843
11/16/2013	$7.00	$5.40	$0.09	$0.02	0.9697
11/16/2013	$8.00	$4.40	$0.09	$0.02	0.9516
11/16/2013	$9.00	$3.50	$0.19	$0.02	0.9082
11/16/2013	$10.00	$2.59	$0.28	$0.02	0.8376
11/16/2013	$11.00	$1.82	$0.51	$0.02	0.7302
11/16/2013	$12.00	$1.18	$0.87	$0.02	0.5876

If you were interested in purchasing 1,000 shares of Bank of America at $12.31 but were intrigued by the possibility of using the stock replacement strategy of buying deep-in-the-money call options, this option chain offers some appealing choices. The first of the four criteria is a strike price that is significantly in-the-money. There are several such possibilities among the November 2013 expiring options. The second of the four criteria suggests a delta of at least 0.90. That eliminates the $10, $11, and $12 strike prices, all of which would be eliminated under the first criterion as well. Third, there should be very little time value associated with the call option. That rule shifts my focus to the $3, $4, $5, and $6 strike prices, all of which have the same and the lowest time values of the group. The deltas among those four are also quite similar and adequate, ranging from 0.9843 to 0.9916. So which of the four is the best choice?

At this point, you should already know whether you plan to leverage the position. If you do not plan to leverage the position, the $6 strike price seems like a good choice. It is deep-in-the-money, is tied for the lowest time value, has a delta that is quite sufficient, and would cost you the least of the $3, $4, $5, and $6 strike prices. A 1,000 share purchase of Bank of America at $12.31 would cost $12,310 before commissions. By purchasing the $6 deep-in-the-money calls, you would only pay $6,350 before commissions ($6.35 offer price × 10 contracts × 100 shares = $6,350). Moreover, with a delta of .9843, should Bank of America's stock rise, you would track its price performance nearly one for one. Should the stock fall below $6 prior to expiration, you would not lose more than the amount paid for the call options, unlike shareholders who would continue to lose money below $6 per share. On the downside, however, you would have paid a bit extra for the call options in the form of $0.04 in time value and the fact that you would miss two dividend payments of $0.01 each. If the $0.06 of non-intrinsic value premium concerns you, consider investing the nearly $6,000 you would have saved from buying call options rather than shares of the company in a CD that expires around option expiration day.

On the same day that you could purchase the $6 November 16, 2013 expiring Bank of America call option for $6.35, you could have also purchased GE Capital certificates of deposit (CDs) in the secondary market, expiring on 10/15/2013, at an annual yield of 0.652% (CUSIP 36160TRP3). That CUSIP, held for just under six months, would help cover the yield you would have paid in premiums on the Bank of America call options ($0.06 / $12.31 = 0.49%). There were also plenty of other CDs trading on the secondary market that would help cover the combined premium from time value and dividends on the call options.

On the other hand, if you do want to leverage the deep-in-the-money calls, you should not purchase the $6 call options. Instead, you need to follow the fourth of the aforementioned criteria, which reads as follows: "If you are interested in leveraging in the manner previously discussed, the strike price of the call option should be so far in-the-money that the odds of the price of the underlying security falling below it are very small." Even though the $6 strike price is significantly in-the-money, it is not far enough in-the-money that I would be extremely confident it would stay that way. The $4 strike price would make me more comfortable because it is below the major support level from 2011. During that year, Bank of America's stock looked like it was headed back to its 2009 low under $3 per share. But it did not get that far, instead bottoming at $4.92 on December 19, 2011.

Why would I not choose the $3 strike, the lowest strike price available, and the closest strike price to the 2009 low? The reason is partially a function of time to expiration (just under seven months between April 24, 2013 and November 2013's expiration) and a function of wanting to pay a low enough premium that the position can be sufficiently leveraged. The $4 strike price seemed like a happy medium. If, however, the expiration date under consideration were much further out in time, such as the January 2015 expiring options, more consideration would certainly be given to the $3 strike price.

To purchase ten of the November 16, 2013 expiring $4 call options (representing 1,000 shares) for $8.35 would cost $8,350 before commissions. This compares to the $12,310 it would cost before commissions to purchase 1,000 shares of Bank of America at $12.31. With the additional $3,960 saved from not buying shares of Bank of America, you could purchase an additional four call options at a cost of $3,340 before commissions. That would increase your exposure to 1,400 shares (14 contracts) and bring your total cost to $11,690 before commissions. With the leveraged position, it would take very little of a rise in Bank of America's share price to more than make up for the $0.06 in time value and dividends missed.

Let's now move on to a discussion of taxes and risks associated with both leveraged and unleveraged deep-in-the-money call option positions used as a stock replacement strategy. But before doing so, I would like to remind readers that Bank of America was chosen purely as an example to help you think through the process of creating a deep-in-the-money call option position. The example was not meant to be an endorsement of Bank of America's stock or its options as an investment.

Taxes

This is what the IRS has to say regarding taxes for holders (those who purchased) of options (wording directly quoted from "IRS Publication 550: Investment Income and Expenses"):

1. If you buy a put or a call, you may not deduct its cost. It is a capital expenditure.

2. If you sell the put or the call before you exercise it, the difference between its cost and the amount you receive for it is either a long-term or short-term capital gain or loss, depending on how long you held it.

3. If the option expires, its cost is either a long-term or short-term capital loss, depending on your holding period, which ends on the expiration date.

4. If you exercise a call, add its cost to the basis of the stock you bought. If you exercise a put, reduce your amount realized on the sale of the underlying stock by the cost of the put when figuring your gain or loss. Any gain or loss on the sale of the underlying stock is long term or short term depending on your holding period for the underlying stock.

Regarding these four rules, there are three things I would like to mention. First, holders of call options can have their capital gains qualify for favorable long-term rates, assuming holding period requirements are met. From a tax perspective, this puts investors using the stock replacement strategy on a level playing field with shareholders of the underlying stock.

Second, should you ever decide to exercise your right, as a holder of call options, to purchase shares of the underlying stock, you need to add the cost of the options to the basis of the stock you bought. In other words, if you paid $30 per contract for a call option with a $50 strike price, and then exercised the option, your cost basis in shares of the underlying would be $80 ($30 + $50) plus commissions.

Third, if you exercise a call option and purchase shares of the underlying security, your holding period resets. Rule number two makes it very clear that selling an *option* you own results in a long-term or short-term capital gain or loss, depending on how long you held the *option*. Rule number four makes it quite clear that if you exercise a call option, any long-term or short-term gain or loss on the shares you purchased is determined based on your holding period for the underlying stock. Moreover, according to a different part of Publication 550, "Your holding period for property you acquire when you exercise an option begins the day after you exercise the option." Keep this in mind if you have held an option for more than one year and are thinking about exercising it.

Risks

There are several risks I would like to address. I will start with those applicable to both leveraged and unleveraged deep-in-the-money calls. When purchasing options, you will likely pay for some amount of time value built into the option premium, even when purchasing ultra-deep-in-the-money calls. When leveraging the position, should the price of the underlying security rise, you can easily make up for the time value paid with profits from the extra call options purchased. This is because your total exposure to the underlying is bigger than it would have been had you only purchased shares. In an unleveraged position, however, you cannot do this. Instead, you might consider thinking about the time value built into the option premium as the cost of ensuring that should the stock plunge below your strike price, you would not lose as much money as shareholders of the underlying security would (your losses are capped at the premium paid for the options).

Second, if the delta is not equal to 1, you will not keep up with shares of the underlying security on a penny for penny basis. Third, as the owner of call options, you are not entitled to receive dividends paid to shareholders of the underlying security. Depending on the size of the dividend, a leveraged position can make up for missing dividend payments. But unleveraged positions do not have that luxury. This is why, when using deep-in-the-money call options as a stock replacement strategy, you should consider focusing on stocks that do not pay dividends, stocks that pay dividends less frequent than quarterly, and stocks that have very low dividend yields.

Finally, you should be aware that it is not unusual for deep-in-the-money options to have bid prices (the price at which you would sell) that are too low relative to where the stock is trading. What do I mean by "too low"? If XYZ stock is trading at $50 per share, and the $25 call option is bidding $24.90, that is too low. In other words, selling at $24.90 would be the equivalent of selling the stock at $49.90 ($25 + $24.90). But the stock is trading at $50. In this case, you should consider exercising the calls and immediately selling the shares at the higher price (assuming doing so would not cause you to lose a "long-term" holding period as previously discussed). Of course, you would need enough capital to do so. If you leveraged the position, you might not have the capital available to exercise the calls and instead would be forced to sell the options at the lower price.

If you find yourself in a situation in which you do not have the funds available to exercise the calls and instead must close the position by selling the call options, keep this in mind. Often, deep-in-the-money options have bid-ask spreads that are fairly wide. The bid-ask spread refers to the difference between the bid price and the ask price. Using the example from the previous paragraph, on a $25 call option with an underlying security trading at $50, it would not surprise me to see a bid-ask spread of $24.90 by $25.10. In that case, you might consider searching for hidden liquidity and entering a sell-to-close order at $24.95. I have been filled many times at prices between the bid price and the ask price. If you do not feel a desperate rush to exit your position, it is worth taking a chance and trying to get filled at a slightly better price.

Concerning spreads on deep-in-the-money options, I have also seen spreads so wide that you should consider avoiding the options altogether. An example of this might be a stock trading at $50 with a call option at the $25 strike price bidding $22 and asking $27. In those cases, you can certainly search for hidden liquidity. But when doing so, remember that you will likely need to find hidden liquidity at attractive prices on two occasions: once on the buy order and once on the sell order.

Turning more specifically to leveraged deep-in-the-money call positions (leveraged as described in this chapter, not leveraged with borrowed money), there is one risk in particular I would like to point out: If the price of the underlying security is below your strike price on expiration, you will not only lose more money than an unleveraged position, but you will also likely lose more money than shareholders of the underlying security. This is because you will have taken the extra funds saved by buying deep-in-the-money calls, instead of having bought shares of the underlying, and used those funds to purchase even more call options.

Earlier in this chapter, I presented a hypothetical example of leveraging a call options position with a $40 strike price on a stock trading at $75 per share. In the example, a leveraged investor could end up with double the exposure to XYZ than an unleveraged investor or a shareholder. But by doubling the exposure, the leveraged investor could lose significantly more money should XYZ fall below the $40 strike price. If you ever plan to leverage an options position in the manner described in this chapter, it is imperative that you choose a strike price that, under any type of reasonably foreseeable circumstance, would not be broken to the downside.

Additionally, when leveraging a deep-in-the-money call option, remember that you will need an even greater amount of funds set aside in order to exercise the calls. If exercising the calls is something you never plan to do, than this would be of no concern.

* * * * *

The first three options strategies presented focused on generating income and capital appreciation for a portfolio. Now it is time to discuss how to protect an investment using options. Since the 2007 to 2009 financial crisis, many investors have shifted their focus from a return *on* their capital to a return *of* their capital. This shift in focus has likely even kept some investors from enjoying the incredible returns equity indices provided in the years immediately following the 2009 lows. If you are generally reluctant to purchase stocks because of the fear of losing money, the last of the four options strategies every investor should know may be of interest. I call it the "get out of jail free" card, and, although it cannot rectify all types of equity market declines, it is a handy strategy to save for a rainy day.

Chapter 6

Your "Get out of Jail Free" Card

For those with a previous familiarity of options, when hearing about a strategy for protecting against losses, you may have immediately thought of protective puts. While buying put options to protect against further downside in the price of the underlying security does have a role in the strategy I am about to describe, the ultimate goal of the strategy is to exit a position with no losses. Buying put options alone, in the way that most investors use protective puts, only limits your losses.

In the world of options, there is a strategy called a *collar*, which involves owning shares of an underlying security, selling a covered call against that security, and purchasing protective put options. Typically, an equal number of out-of-the-money puts and calls are purchased and sold, and the premium collected from the covered call is used to reduce the premium paid for the protective puts. If you execute this strategy in the traditional way, you are still likely to be left with a loss on your position.

While I think learning to accept losses is a critical component of long-term investing success, an element of learning to accept losses is also recognizing when a loss should be taken. You may discover that it is worthwhile to attempt to exit the position without a loss, using a variant of the traditional options collar strategy.

Construction of the Position

The modified collar I will describe can be used to exit a position on which you have an unrealized loss but at the same time are not convinced that realizing the loss is a necessary action. It is ideal for times when the decline in the price of the underlying security is only minor to moderate, but you are not confident the security will return to your cost basis at any point in the foreseeable future. If you have the patience to use options over a period of many months, you can use the modified collar to slowly eliminate your position without taking any losses.

How will the collar (long the underlying, short a call, long a put) be modified from the traditional form? Instead of buying and selling an equal number of options, the modified collar will take the premium from the covered call and use only that premium (not a penny more) to purchase as many put options as possible on the underlying security. This is different than the typical construction of a collar, which purchases an equal amount of put options, even if that results in a net debit from an investor's portfolio. Unlike in a typical collar, which usually leaves some potential for profit, while also leaving open the possibility for a loss, the modified collar has a first priority of preventing losses, and only a second priority of realizing small gains.

For example, let's pretend you attempted to pick a bottom in XYZ after it fell from $30 to $23 per share. After purchasing 1,000 shares of XYZ, the stock continued to decline, falling to $21. At that point, you would have an unrealized loss of $2 per share or 8.70%. If the continued decline made you realize your position is simply too large or caused you to fear the price might not get back to your cost basis, you might consider looking at the call and put premiums at the $23 strike price and creating a collar. If the $23 put options expiring in three months were offered at $3.45, and the $23 call options expiring in three months were bidding $1.45, you could put together the following collar:

Sell ten $23 call options (representing your 1,000 shares) for $1.45, collecting $1,450 less commissions. Assuming a commission of $8 plus $0.75 per contract plus a small transaction fee, the net premium collected is roughly $1,434.

Next, use the $1,434 to purchase four $23 put options (representing 400 of your shares) at a price of $3.45. This would cost $1,380 before commissions. Assuming a commission of $8 plus $0.75 per contract, the total premium paid would be $1,391.

Should XYZ close above $23 per share on expiration, the put options would expire worthless, and your shares would be called away from you at your cost basis of $23 (because of the in-the-money covered calls). Depending on your broker's commission schedule, the $43 difference between the call premium collected and the put premium paid should be enough to cover any further commissions from selling XYZ as a result of an options assignment.

If XYZ closes below $23 on expiration, the call options would expire worthless, and you would keep the entire premium of $1,434. The put options would finish in-the-money, and you could exercise the put options, resulting in your selling 400 shares of the position at $23 per share. Depending on your broker's commission schedule, the $43 difference between the call premium collected and the put premium paid should be enough to cover any further commissions from selling 400 shares of XYZ as a result of exercising the puts.

By using the collar strategy as described above, you would either exit your position in whole, with no loss, if the price of XYZ were over $23 on expiration, or reduce the size of your position by 400 shares, with no loss to the 400 shares, should XYZ close anywhere below $23 on expiration. Your total position size in XYZ would drop to 600 shares, and you could then consider the merits of executing the same strategy again.

Next, let's pretend the price of XYZ had continued lower, falling to $20, or 13.04% below your cost basis of $23. As should be expected, the call premiums at the $23 strike price would also fall as the $23 call options became further out-of-the-money. The put premiums, however, would rise in price as they went deeper in-the-money. Now you would be left with a $23 strike price call premium of just $1.10 for options expiring in three months, and a $23 strike price put premium of $4.15 for the options expiring on the same date.

With just 600 shares of your original position remaining, you could sell six $23 call options for $1.10 and collect a net premium (after commissions and a small transaction fee) of roughly $647. The $647 could then be used to purchase just one put option (representing 100 shares) for a cost, after commissions, of $423.75. The remaining $223.25 could be used to offset any further commissions and to potentially enjoy a small profit on the overall position.

Again, should XYZ close above $23 per share on expiration, the put option would expire worthless, and your shares would be called away from you at your cost basis of $23 (because of the in-the-money covered calls). If XYZ were to close below $23 on expiration, the call options would expire worthless, the put option would finish in-the-money, and you could allow the put option to be automatically exercised, resulting in your selling 100 shares of the position at $23 per share.

By once again using the collar strategy, you would either exit your position in whole, with no loss, if the price of XYZ is over $23 on expiration, or reduce the size of your position by 100 shares, with no loss to the 100 shares, should XYZ close anywhere below $23 on expiration. Your total position size in

XYZ would drop to 500 shares, and you could again consider the merits of executing the same strategy.

If you have the patience to continue this strategy over an extended period of time, there is a very good chance of drastically reducing your exposure to XYZ, thereby freeing up capital to use elsewhere while you wait to exit the remainder of the position. An important component to reducing the size of your position using this modified collar is to make the decision early enough in a security's decline that you can exit a significant part of the position on the first try.

Real World Example

In the previous example, the collar that was used to reduce the position size in XYZ stock was executed only after the position was already 8.70% underwater. But as I noted, the earlier you make a decision to exit a position, the better. With that in mind, I will use BHP Billiton, ticker symbol BHP, as an example of how quickly a losing position can be drawn down, without having to take a loss, if you act before the unrealized losses become too great.

On April 25, 2013, BHP's stock closed at $66.56. Throughout the month of April, the price action in the stock was quite choppy and volatile with decent size moves both up and down. Let's pretend you got long 600 shares of the stock at $67.50 on April 8. Less than two months earlier, on February 19, BHP traded as high as $80.54. Even though you felt good about your entry point, you were nervous about the volatility the stock exhibited.

The very next day after you bought shares at $67.50, BHP was trading at $71.46. You felt like a genius. In just one day, you were up more than 5% on your position. But just four trading days later, the stock had reversed course in a big way and closed at $64.77. That was a drop of 9.36% in just a few trading days, erasing your unrealized profits. Three more trading days later, BHP traded as low as $63.19. You went from being up more than 5% on your position to down more than 6% in less than two weeks. Thoughts of "Why didn't I sell at $71?" were running through your head. If only the stock would return to $71, you would get out.

Five trading days later, BHP's stock finally made a run at $67.50 again. Surely this would be the day you got back to even. At 9:37 AM, BHP was trading at $66.55 when suddenly, it was off to the races. A bit more than half an hour later, at 10:08 AM, it reached $67.49, and stopped. Several minutes later it was back down to $67.26. The frustration of being so close to getting back to even was palpable.

You waited, all the while thinking about whether you should reconsider your $71 price target, when all of a sudden, the share price spiked above $67.50. At last, you were back in the black and thinking the stock was heading to $71. But the joy would be short lived. By 11:05 AM, the stock had dropped back below $67.50 for good, closing the day all the way down at $66.56. As the day progressed and your frustration mounted, you decided that the volatility in the stock was too great for you to handle given your position size of 600 shares. The position needed to be reduced, if not eliminated. But you were not yet ready to give up completely and take a loss on the shares. This would be a great time to check the options prices for a possible collar.

At the close of trading, on April 25, 2013, with BHP at $66.56, the June 22, 2013 expiring $67.50 call options were bidding $2.19, and the $67.50 put options, with the same expiration date, could be purchased for $3.20. Selling six call options for $2.19 would result in a premium of $1,314 less commissions. Assuming a commission of $8 plus $0.75 per contract and a small transaction fee, the net premium collected would be approximately $1,301. Using that $1,301, you could purchase four put options at the $67.50 strike for $3.20. The four puts would cost $1,280 plus commissions, resulting in a total cost of approximately $1,291.

If BHP closed above $67.50 two months later on expiration, the puts would expire worthless, and your shares would be called away from you at $67.50. Should the stock close below $67.50 on expiration, the call options would expire worthless (meaning you keep the entire premium) and the four put options would be auto-exercised, reducing your position by 400 shares. In that case, your exposure to the stock would drop from $40,500 ($67.50 × 600 shares) to $13,500 ($67.50 × 200 shares).

Even though you were down on your position (BHP trading at $66.56 versus your cost basis of $67.50), by using the collar, you guaranteed, at worst, a two-thirds reduction in the size of your position for no loss. Some investors might find it foolish not to just take the loss and move on. Others might think you should wait things out to see if the stock will move back above your cost basis before June's option expiration. But for those investors who have the luxury of time and are willing to gradually wind down a position, especially if it means not taking a loss on the full position, the options collar is the way to go.

After all, by not taking any action, the stock could rise back above your cost basis, but it could also fall, thereby increasing your unrealized losses. On the other hand, if you were to sell the 600 shares of BHP immediately, taking a loss on the full position, you would lock in losses of $564 before commissions ($67.50 cost basis - $66.56 stock price = $0.94. $0.94 × 600 shares = $564). If you use the collar, however, to reduce your position to 200 shares, it would take a $2.82 decline in BHP's stock for you to realize a $564 loss. This means the stock would need to decline to $64.68 ($67.50 - $2.82) before you would ever have to worry about whether you should have taken losses on the entire position at $66.56. Even if after June's option expiration, the stock were trading so far below your cost basis that a collar strategy would not work to reduce your position size any more, between the dividends paid over time and the ability to sell covered calls, there would still be an opportunity to make up for any unrealized losses on the remainder of your position.

In the meantime, you could take the $27,000 in capital you freed up ($67.50 × 400 shares sold) from using the collar to reduce your position by 400 shares and continue investing in other opportunities. It is even possible that the profits you would generate from the $27,000 you freed up could offset potential losses from the smaller position remaining in BHP, should the stock not recover to your cost basis.

Taxes

When creating a collar, you have opened yourself up to the tax implications associated with straddles. Publication 550 will detail everything you need to know about straddles and taxes, some of which I have already presented in this book. Beyond what I have already discussed in earlier chapters, the following may come in handy when thinking about the tax consequences of using a collar to protect a portfolio position: When building collars in your portfolio, stick to expiration dates within a calendar year that expire no later than the monthly November options. That gives you eleven months of the year to use collars to protect against losses. If you do this, you should not have any tax complications from rules associated with "straddles."

If, however, you are considering using collars with expiration dates in December or in the following calendar year, and there is a chance you will not hold the options until expiration, familiarize yourself with the "Loss Deferral Rules," including the "Special year-end rule" for straddles. These can be found in IRS Publication 550. Furthermore, if you are already perusing Publication 550, it is worth reading about the "wash sale" rule. In my opinion, anyone who buys and sells securities in the financial markets should be aware of the "wash sale" rule.

In closing the discussion on taxes, I would like to share one more thought. If taxes are a subject with which you want nothing to do, but you also want to trade options, consider hiring someone to worry about the tax implications for you. That will leave you to focus your efforts on other things. Alternatively, you could trade options in a tax-advantaged account and not have to worry about options-related tax rules at all.

Risks

Even though the title of this chapter is "Your 'Get out of Jail Free' Card," there are risks associated with creating a collar to help you wind down a losing position. The biggest risk is that the stock you own keeps going down, falling dramatically below your cost basis. In that case, you will find it quite difficult to reduce your position size in any meaningful way without incurring losses. If you think there is a reasonably high likelihood of a significant drop in the price of a stock you own, then you should not consider using the strategy discussed in this chapter. Instead, you should consider selling your position or buying enough puts to protect against your entire position declining.

Another risk concerns not owning enough shares of the underlying security to make the strategy a viable one. If you only own a few hundred shares of a stock, it will be difficult to wind down that position using the strategy discussed in this chapter. If, however, you own a few thousand shares, then the strategy becomes more attractive.

Third, stocks that have illiquid option chains and wide bid-ask spreads will make life difficult for an investor wanting to execute the options collar strategy at a fair price.

Fourth, if you find yourself down in a position, and the underlying security is one that typically exhibits low volatility in the share price, you may discover that the option premiums on out-of-the-money calls are so low that the collar strategy will only work to a small degree. In that case, you might consider selling a moderately deep-in-the-money call option to stem your losses. The formula for doing so is the following:

Strike Price + Covered Call Premium Collected = Cost Basis of Your Shares

If you can sell an in-the-money covered call at a premium that when added to the strike price (the price at which you would sell shares) is equal to or greater than your cost basis, you will end up either hedging your position in a meaningful way or eliminating the unrealized losses altogether. It all depends on the price of the underlying security at expiration.

* * * * *

As it pertains to investing, I agree with the often recited phrase, "There is no such thing as a free lunch." Risks are ubiquitous in the world of investing, and the strategy discussed in this chapter is no exception.

CHAPTER 7

What About Other Options Strategies?

There are numerous options strategies I could have written about in this book. Some readers might be wondering how I could have left "married puts" off the list. Married puts, also known as protective puts, protect investors from drops in the underlying security. A married put combines a long position in the underlying security with a long position in the underlying's put options.

I also left credit spreads and debit spreads off the list of options strategies every investor should know. A credit spread involves buying and selling options at the same time so that the net result to the portfolio is a credit. A debit spread also involves buying and selling options at the same time so that the net result to the portfolio is a debit. There are reasons for doing each of these trades, and those reasons were beyond the scope of this book.

Moreover, I did not discuss options strategies that can be used to profit from declines in equity prices. This could involve buying deep-in-the-money puts or even selling naked call options. An investor could also have an outright short position in the underlying security and sell puts against the position. This is called a covered put position. It is essentially the same thing as a covered call position, but instead of being long the underlying and selling a call option, you are short the underlying and selling a put option. An investor who is short a stock might also buy call options to hedge the position. This is called a "married call." In terms of hedging, this is along the same lines as those investors who are long a stock and buy a put option to hedge (married put position).

There is even an options strategy that provides investors a very high likelihood of being able to purchase the underlying security at a price that is lower than the market is currently offering. It involves strategically selling deep-in-the-money puts at a strike price you are reasonably certain will result in an assignment of the underlying security, at a cost basis lower than the underlying is then-currently trading.

Finally, I could have included a variety of options straddles and options strangles in this book. Investors can initiate long straddles positions and short straddles positions depending on how much they expect the underlying security to move. There are also long and short strangle positions an investor can trade. The list of different options strategies available to investors is a long one. So why did I choose the ones I did?

Before I answer that question, I would first like to state that I am a big believer that each investor's situation is unique to that individual. Each of us will have our own risk tolerance, time horizons, and investment objectives, which will differ, even if only slightly, from everyone else's. With that said, the four options strategies discussed in this book address three investing goals that most, if not all, investors have in common: generating income, capital appreciation, and downside protection.

My goal was to introduce options strategies that investors of every type would find helpful, actionable, and relatively easy to understand. I also wanted the strategies to be implementable without the need for a margin account. Finally, I wanted the list to include only low- or zero-cost strategies with which investors would avoid having to pay large premiums above the intrinsic value of the option. That is why I left married puts off the list.

The first two strategies, covered call writing and selling cash-secured puts, are income generating methods that are simple in their construction. Buying deep-in-the-money calls is a way for investors with strong convictions to initiate a type of leveraged long position without the need for borrowing on margin or paying large premiums in excess of an option's intrinsic value. If correct in their convictions, those investors would be able to realize larger capital appreciation than they would by purchasing the stock outright. The final strategy helps investors reduce the size of a losing position without having to realize losses on that position. No matter what type of investor you are, you should, at the very least, be aware of these strategies in case the time ever comes that you need to or want to rely on one.

With this book, I also wanted to challenge the stereotype of options as only being risky, dangerous, speculative, overly complex, and the domain of gamblers. I hope that with the four strategies outlined in this book, you have a new appreciation for options as sensible, helpful, risk-reducing, protective, and income-enhancing investment vehicles. Despite what you may hear or read, options do not have to be the scary, ultra-dangerous speculative venture they are made out to be. Options trading cannot be adequately described in broad strokes. There are many different types of options strategies, and they cover a large part of the risk spectrum.

Among all available options strategies, four in particular stand out to me as useful tools for helping investors of all types achieve their investment goals: covered calls, cash-secured puts, deep-in-the-money calls as a stock replacement strategy, and one specific type of options collar. As you navigate the choppy investing waters of the world's financial markets, I hope the four options strategies presented in this book serve you well.

Good luck and happy investing!

About the Author

The Financial Lexicon has spent more than a decade in the financial world and has extensive experience trading and investing in equities, options, fixed income, and alternative investment products. If you would like to read more by The Financial Lexicon, visit LearnBonds.com, SeekingAlpha.com, or read the book *The 5 Fundamentals of Building a Retirement Portfolio*.

Made in the USA
Lexington, KY
25 July 2013